Children and Christian Initiation: A Practical Guide to the Catechumenate

Kathy Coffey

Living the Good News, Inc.
Denver, CO
in cooperation with
The North American Forum
on the Catechumenate

Table of Contents

Living the Good News, Inc.
600 Grant Street, Suite 400
Denver, CO 80203

Printed in the United States of America
Illustrations: Anne Kosel
Cover Photographs: Mark Kiryluk

ISBN 0-8192-8002-X

Introduction:
Looking Back, Looking Forward

You have embarked on a journey. The journey started in the period called precatechumenate when you began to companion a child through the process of initiation. The ultimate goal of the journey is full initiation through the sacraments of baptism, confirmation and eucharist. This book is a guide for the second period, called the catechumenate.

Your role may be that of a parent, catechist, team member, sponsor, godparent or supportive member of the Christian community. You know that children today face stresses and problems that were unimagined a generation ago. You also believe that giving them the companionship of Jesus and the faith treasured by the Catholic tradition will help them through difficult times.

Although you may not be ready to admit it, you are serving as a channel of God's grace to this child. To the abstract notion of a caring God, you give human flesh. Your touch, your laughter, your listening ear, your honestly shared doubt, your wink, your generously given time clearly communicate that God loves the child mightily. You may have questions or worries, which are natural, but most of all, you want to serve this child or these children well.

Looking Back

During the period of precatechumenate, your task was to welcome, befriend and listen. The child's questions were the starting point. Perhaps those questions prompted you to think about your own faith and to re-examine it in a new light. The old adage says that we can't give what we don't have. So during the precatechumenate, you reflected on the image of God and the kinds of prayer you want to pass on to this child.

You also became familiar with some of the components of the initiation process: its call for parental and family involvement, its emphasis on liturgical catechesis, prayer and service. You may have observed that a child learns more from the people he or she models than from any text-book. Finally, you participated in the rite of acceptance or welcome.

Many people find that signing their child with the cross during that rite is a profoundly moving experience. The children feel the same way. "I felt strong," said Andy. Mike agreed: "When my parents bent down to sign my feet, it's like they were saying they would be loyal to me. I just felt like I was the big person." "It could also be," Keesha mused about the signing on her feet, "that if you score a goal in soccer, it's like Jesus was there to help you." Her dad echoed her idea: "Since we started this process Jesus seems to be more present in our family." That is a fine foundation on which to build.

Looking Forward

During the catechumenate period, you and the child may have many eye-opening experiences. You will break open the word or study the Sunday scriptures. You will experience rites in which the church, like a mother, strengthens her children with God's blessing. As you and your child focus more on Christ, you may see subtle changes in behavior. Don't worry: neither you nor the child will become prissy or pious. But hold on tight: you and the child may become more loving, more prayerful, more generous, even at the cost of self-sacrifice. It's a funny thing about spending this time with Jesus, getting to know him through story and symbol. He has the power to transform...

The Catechumenate Period

"In the effort to give good and comforting answers to
the young questioners whom we love, we very often
arrive at good and comforting answers for ourselves."
—Ruth Goode

Liturgical Catechesis

At the heart of this period is formation by the word and the minor rites.
Usually, children are dismissed from the Sunday assembly to break open
the word or explore the scripture readings. Their catechetical session will
always include a blessing done by the catechist and at times, minor exor-
cisms and anointings that flow from the scriptures. This method is called
liturgical catechesis.

Let's review the definition of liturgical catechesis, since it is new to many
people and essential to this period. The term combines two words:
* liturgy—from the official public worship of the church, especially
  eucharist and the sacraments.
* catechesis—from the Greek word "to sound down" or "re-echo," the
  formation and guidance that trains children in the Christian way of life.

The two terms together combine the best of both liturgy and catechesis.
The enhanced faith experience that results has the power to convert and
transform the person. Liturgical catechesis is powerful because it appeals
not only to the intellect, but also to the heart and the imagination. The
whole person is involved; it invites the child's intrinsic sense of wonder
to flower.

Using this approach is not a new gimmick, but a return to an older order.
Illiterate people of the middle ages could not learn the faith from books.

They absorbed it from the people and the symbols around them: the stained glass windows that told the story of Jesus' life, the chant ascending to the Gothic arches of their cathedrals.

This example from Sigrid Undset's novel *Kristin Lavransdatter* describes the awe of a young girl named Kristin, seeing for the first time the windows of a medieval Norwegian cathedral. Her guide is a monk who helps her climb the scaffolding:

> Upon the greystone wall above her Kristin saw wondrous fluttering flecks of light; red as blood and yellow as beer, blue and brown and green. She would have turned to look behind her, but the monk whispered, "Turn not about." But when they stood together high upon the planking, he turned her gently round, and Kristin saw a sight so fair she almost lost her breath.

> Right over against her on the nave's south wall stood a picture, and it shone as if it were made of naught but gleaming precious stones. The many-hued flecks of light upon the wall came from rays which stood out from that picture; she herself and the monk stood in the midst of the glory...

> 'Twas like standing far off and looking into the heavenly kingdom. Behind a network of black streaks, she made out little by little the Lord Christ Himself in the most precious of red robes, the Virgin Mary in raiment blue as heaven, holy men and maidens in shining yellow and green and violet array...

> "Stand here," [the monk] whispered, "and [it will] shine right upon you from Christ's own robe."

Today, children are lured by the messages of the media, presented with dazzling audio-visual effects. The riches of the church can communicate with similar drama: through story and rite that appeal to the imagination and the sense of wonder. Like Kristin, our children can stand bathed in the light reflected from Christ's red robe.

Purpose of the Period
The goals of this second period are to deepen faith by:

- celebrating the rites
- studying the scriptures
- entering the community's life of prayer and service.

Again the emphasis is on the child's growing personal friendship with God, not on the information about God he or she may be acquiring. A good motto for this period might be: "Faith is caught, not taught."

Personal Goals
Reflecting on the Past
What do these guidelines mean for you, the child's parent, godparent, catechist or sponsor?

Let's begin with an admission of past failures in faith formation. Somehow, many people who had an essentially academic training did not develop the personal relationship with Jesus that is at the heart of faith. If the old approaches failed then, they are even likelier to fail the children of a much more unsettled era.

Jim Dunning, founder of the North American Forum on the Catechumenate, includes these statistics in his book *Echoing God's Word* (p. 12):
- A Gallup poll showed Catholics scoring lowest in agreeing with the statement, "God loves you a great deal," and in believing they have a personal relationship with God.
- Dean Hoge's research uncovered the fact that 38 percent of all priests and 55 percent of people in the 55–65 age bracket say faith is "belief in the doctrines of the Catholic Church."

Father Dunning interprets the statistics as a sad commentary on "a dead faith" that makes doctrine and law more important than a personal relationship with God in community. Always, faith, kindness, mercy and the Spirit of God come first. Then come doctrine, law, behavior and tradition.

Reflect on this question in writing, in silence or with a partner:
- What can I do during this process so that this child, if asked "Does God love you a great deal?" would answer with a resounding "Yes!"

If your answer to the question includes something about loving the child so that he or she knows God loves him or her, you're on the right track.

You are a vital channel for the love of God in this child's life. Remember the story of the little girl afraid of the dark, who called out to her mother for help? Her mother, tired and frustrated called back, "Pray to God about your fear!" The child wailed, "But I want a God with skin!" The doctrine of the incarnation teaches us that in Bethlehem, God took on human skin. And ever since, God has been present in human beings. The Jesuit poet Gerard Manley Hopkins puts it this way:

> Christ plays in ten thousand places,
> Lovely in limbs, and lovely in eyes not his
> To the Father through the features of men's faces.

The letter of John says it in a similar way:

> Whoever does not love does not know God, for God is love...
> Those who say, "I love God," and hate their brothers and sisters, are liars; for those who do not love a brother or sister whom they have seen, cannot love God whom they have not seen (1 John 4:8, 20).

Reflecting on the Present

God is an abstraction to children. They know God through the loving adults and children they encounter. Do our actions and attitudes reveal an angry, punitive God or a warm, caring God, anxious to embrace children? Without good modeling, children may not know what love looks like. Your example can help them to love God and other people.

Children's natural longing for God has become more intense as stresses on them increase. When their lives seem chaotic, they turn to God to bring meaning. When a barrage of social changes assaults their security, they find refuge in God's unchanging care. When their self-esteem is weakened or destroyed, they are buoyed by God's assurance that they are beloved daughters and sons. For example, Tyrese is a shy child whose cousin was stabbed to death. He finds life without God unimaginable, "because who would you trust?"

If you are feeling inadequate about this role as sacrament of God's presence to the child, remember that you do not act alone, but with God. The child longs for infinite love. God is the source of that unconditional love. Sofia Cavalletti, author of *The Religious Potential of the Child*, said in an interview: "The best mother and the best father have their limits, after all. With God the children have found the right partner for them."

A Prayer As You Begin

The Book of Hosea describes God as this tender parent and partner. Read this passage slowly and reflectively, substituting the name of your child where the Bible refers to Israel or Ephraim, and if your child is female, changing the word "son" to "daughter." Since Egypt was a place of slavery for the Jews, you might change the word "Egypt" to the word "slavery." Reflect on the ways God has already acted in this child's life. Pray that you might continue to enflesh the tender compassion of God as you act in God's image. God speaks in this passage with a parent's love:

When Israel was a child, I loved him,
and out of Egypt I called my son.
The more I called them, the more they went from me...
Yet it was I who taught Ephraim to walk,
I took them up in my arms;
but they did not know that I healed them.
I led them with cords of human kindness,
with bands of love.
I was to them like those who lift infants to their cheeks.
I bent down to them and fed them.   —Hosea 11:1-4

You may even want to use this passage in a prayer service for all the team members, sponsors and parents in the initiation process. As each person substitutes names, it may sound something like this:

When Katie was a child, I loved her,
and out of slavery I called my daughter...

Timing

This period of catechumenate is marked by two threshold rites: the rite of acceptance or welcome at the beginning and the rite of election at the end.

The length of time a child spends in this period depends entirely on the child's needs. It should be long enough for the child's faith to become strong. For some children, it may last several years. Thus, there is no rush to "complete" the catechumenate. As the person in the process who probably knows the child best, you may be asked to discern the child's readiness for the rite of election, which will declare that this child is eternally chosen by God and ready to make final preparation for the sacraments of initiation.

Discerning Readiness for the Rite of Election

Looking toward the end of this period, be alert for the signs of conversion in a child. Rita Burns Senseman of Nobelsville, Indiana, gives this definition and suggests that conversion has four dimensions:

• Conversion means a change of heart, a change in lifestyle and attitudes, a turning toward Jesus Christ.

Affective

The child moves from cognitive or "head" knowledge of God to a felt personal relationship with God.

Social

The child moves from seeing him or herself as an individual ("Tuan") or a family member ("Nguyen") to seeing him or herself as part of the larger Christian community ("Holy Redeemer Parish").

Intellectual

This does not mean that children master the whole body of Christian doctrine, but that they have "a sense of the mystery of salvation." Burns Senseman cites the example of Sandra, who after being signed with the cross at the rite of acceptance or welcome said, "It felt like Jesus was covering me. He is on my head, and hands, and eyes and ears. It's like he is surrounding me. I feel like he'll always be there for me."

Moral

This is the child's personal response of giving self to others: doing kindnesses at home and school, participating in service projects, contributing in whatever ways he or she can to his or her community.

Here are some questions, adapted from James Lopresti's discernment for adults that you and the child might talk about together:

• Is there a difference between now and when you started the catechumenate in the way you feel about:
   — God?
   — yourself?
   — your family?
   — your friends?
   — the Catholic Church?
   — your parish?

To simplify this, ask:
- How did the world look to you before you began this process? How does it look now?

Remember, as Maureen Kelly points out, during the rite of election, the presider never asks, "how much doctrine does the child know?" Instead, the questions concern the child's participation in the life of the community, prayer, service and dedication to the word.

Don't be surprised if a child who appears to have been daydreaming expresses a profound insight as you discuss readiness. For instance, Matthew was a rough-and-tumble fourth grader who spent most of his time during initiation sessions fiddling with his baseball cap. Yet when the initiation director asked Matt what he'd been learning, he assured her solemnly, "I know that the angel asked Mary to do whatever God wanted. She did. And now I'm ready to do whatever God wants me to do."

Baseball cap askew, Matt was ready for the rite of election.

Chapter
2

Expanding the Catechumenate Sessions

And find the thin small fingers in the cold,
And touch, and hold.
> —Bianca Bradbury

As you know, the process of initiation is greatly enriched if the formal sessions are expanded by informal follow-up at home. (Doesn't the child who plays basketball at home after the team practices usually do better?) This chapter contains tips to continue the process on a one-on-one basis with an individual child or a few children.

Preparing for a Session

For example, let's say your child participates in the sample catechumenate session on the call to discipleship, p. 59 in *Children and Christian Initiation: A Practical Guide*. Before the session, think about your own sense of calling. This does not mean a dramatic vision or St. Paul being knocked off his horse and blinded by Christ. It may mean a quiet fidelity: to this child, this job, this family. It may mean welcoming the gifts and challenges of each day as if they were sent specially by God to you.

Woody Allen says, "Half of life is just showing up." Explain to the child that the reason you show up, the reason you get out of bed in the morning is that God calls you to a special work no one else has. As you explain your commitment to this particular family, grocery store, garden, car repair business or parish, encourage the child to think about where he or she may feel called.

During the Session

Children hear the story of Jesus calling Peter, Andrew, James and John away from their fishing nets. He promised them they would fish for people instead. Children think about their own sense of being called. They have the option of completing a list called "Why me?" On it they name their gifts and the ways these might be used to serve God.

Follow up

Depending on the child, you may take several different directions after the session. The following list of possibilities ranges from those requiring minimal time to those requiring more. Keep in mind that you may be able to squeeze in a chat with the child as you drive to school or ride the bus together, shop for groceries, wash dishes, fold laundry or prepare for bed:

- Read other stories about people being called to discipleship. Some in scripture are: Abraham (Genesis 12:1-9), Samuel (1 Samuel 3:1-21), Mary (Luke 1:26-38), Matthew (Luke 5:27-32), the Samaritan woman (John 4:1-42).
- Tell stories from your own tradition: for instance, Rosa Parks, Ruby Bridges and Martin Luther King Jr. being called by God for a special role in the civil rights movement; Rigoberta Menchu calling an oppressive Guatemalan government to account for their atrocities against indigenous peoples; Cesar Chavez asserting the rights of migrant workers. If your friends or family members have followed a calling from God, invite them to tell their stories. Then ask the child, "What did you hear about God's call in the story?"
- Hang a shoe in a prominent place, maybe over the kitchen table or the bathroom mirror. Use it as a reminder to "walk in the shoes of Jesus" and to prompt discussion of what that means.
- Cut a shoe shape from construction paper and ask the child to write or draw on it the things he or she does to imitate Jesus or walk in his shoes.
- If your child began the list called "Why me?" in the session, continue to expand it, perhaps by including other family members. If the child did not start the list, simply create two columns on a piece of paper, one marked "my talents" and one marked "God calls me." In the first column the child writes or draws special gifts. In the second, the child writes or draws things God has called him or her to do in the past or may be asking in the future. Respond to the list with comments like this:
  — "I'm glad you listed your sense of humor. I like that in you too—it always cheers up people who are down."

- — "And what about your patience with younger kids? Don't forget to list that..."
- — "You also have a special gift for thwacking a baseball..."
- Explore the question "Who is Jesus?"
  - — Ask the child to tell you, write down or draw everything he or she knows for sure about Jesus.
  - — Add the things he or she doesn't know for sure, but guesses to be true.
  - — Ask the child to tell a favorite story about Jesus. Ask other family members, friends or other children to tell their favorite stories too. You may want to put these together in a hand-made book (pages stapled together or tied with yarn, construction paper cover) with a title such as "The Sanchez Family's Stories of Jesus."

Each week, follow up the child's session by asking about the scriptures of that week. Invite the child to re-echo the word by asking:
- Tell me the story.
- What did you especially like in the story?
- Do you want to draw a picture of it?
- What did the story call you to do this week?

Chapter
3

The Rites and Prayers of the Catechumenate

Teacher to the end.
No worries
if you forget
the words, mate.
Recall the gesture.
—Michael Moynahan, S.J.

This period is marked by two threshold rites: the rite of acceptance or welcome at the beginning, the rite of election at the end. Reflection after the rite of acceptance or welcome appears in *Children and Christian Initiation: A Practical Guide to the Precatechumenate*, page 38. Reading the following section will help you feel fully prepared for the rite of election, in which you may play an important part.

Rite of Election

This rite is usually celebrated within Mass at the beginning of Lent and marks the start of the final preparations for the sacraments of initiation. On the basis of adult testimony and the children's reaffirmation of their intention, the church makes its "election," or choice of the children who will become fully initiated. The importance of this rite is the declaration that God's choice of these children is eternal.

The rite of election usually occurs at the cathedral or another large central location. At the rite of election, candidates and catechumens from all over the diocese assemble. In a large diocese, the rite may be held in several locations to accommodate large numbers of people.

While such numbers may seem overwhelming to a child, the gathering also presents a wonderful opportunity. The child has been bonding with the people of one parish, but he or she may not have been exposed to the universality of the Catholic Church. Seeing that Catholics come in all colors, shapes and sizes can give a sense of that broad dimension. Many parishes hold a potluck back at home base when everyone has returned from the rite of election, because it's a good chance to celebrate unity in diversity.

The optional rite of sending occurs within a smaller parish assembly, usually after the homily at Mass. It is an opportunity for the local community to pray for those being initiated and sent to the rite of election.

In preparation for the rites of sending and election, discuss the child's choice of godparent(s), who accompanies the child on the day of election, at the celebration of the sacraments of initiation and during mystagogy. This godmother and/or godfather shows the child how to live a gospel way of life. They are chosen for their good example, good qualities and friendship. While a parent may be a sponsor, a parent cannot also be a godparent.

Some possible godparents are:
• a grandparent
• an older sibling who has already completed the sacraments of initiation
• the parent of a child's friend

Also in preparation, be familiar with the main parts of the rite:
• Children are presented by a representative of the community.
• Parents, godparents and the assembly give their affirmation of the children.
• The children enroll their names in the book of the elect.
• The celebrant declares the children to be the elect of God, chosen to be initiated at Easter.

Called by Name
The rite begins with a director or catechist presenting the children who ask to be admitted to the sacraments of initiation. The celebrant then calls each child by name, to come forward with parents and godparents.

Each person's name has a special and unique importance because each person is special and unique. Several activities can reinforce that idea. Try one or more, before or after the rite:

- Read biblical stories of name change: for instance, Abram to Abraham and Sarai to Sarah, Simon to Peter, Saul to Paul. Talk about the change of name representing a change of life.
- Talk with the child about how his or her name was chosen. Some parents are very careful about the fit. One mom, meeting her baby daughter in the delivery room, said, "I knew at once she didn't look like a Mary Elizabeth. She looked like a Molly." So Molly she became.
- If the child is named for a relative, does he or she know this person well? If not, what can he or she discover? If this person is dead or lives elsewhere, could a picture, a tape, a story or a memory help bring him or her alive for the child?
- If the child doesn't know the meaning of his or her name, books on naming a baby usually provide this information: for example, David means "beloved"; Lucy means "light."

Affirmation

The celebrant will ask the parents, godparents and assembly these questions:

- Have these children shown themselves to be sincere in their desire for baptism, confirmation and the eucharist?
- Have they listened well to the word of God?
- Have they tried to live as faithful followers?
- Have they taken part in this community's life of prayer and service?

As you prepare for the rite, reflect on these questions with the child. They can help you discern whether or not this child is ready to move ahead at this time or needs more time in the catechumenate.

Some parishes also ask an adult to say a few words on behalf of the child, giving concrete grounding to the ritual statement. If this is the case in your parish, ask the child to help you prepare what you will say to the assembly. If this is not the case in your parish, the following questions might still be helpful for reflection before the rite.

- What are some things you would like people to know about you, Thom?
- How have you grown and changed since you began this process?
- Why do you want to receive baptism-confirmation-eucharist?
- How do you serve and pray with the people of this parish?

Think how often we criticize our children; how seldom we affirm them. This is a chance to correct that imbalance. Before God and the community, proclaim that you are immensely proud of this child. If you're embarrassed about speaking in public or worried that you'll forget your lines, write a few reminders on a small note card, or even on your hand. (After all, God said of the beloved people, "I have carved you on the palm of my hand.") Here's an example of Linda speaking about Raoul. She rested her trembling hands on his arm as she said:

I want you all to know how God is active in the life of this child. I've seen a change in him since he began this process. His relationship with Jesus is making him a kinder person. Every time I see him helping his little sister with homework or running alongside as she learns to ride her bike, my heart brims with pride. When I get home from work and I'm tired, he tells me a joke or rubs my neck. Since he began preparing for initiation, he hasn't missed his day to volunteer at the soup kitchen. I've never seen anyone so hungry to receive the eucharist. I feel blessed to be his mother, and I present him to this community with love and joy.

The words describing God's presence in the child's life can be adapted to fit the person. Try to avoid the generalities ("She's a good kid") and include specifics: ("God has gifted her with the ability to be a graceful dancer and leader of prayer.") Some people feel paralyzed by a church setting, but remember you're talking to family. Don't be afraid to include humor. Sometimes the community is most touched by speech that is halting but heart-felt. For the child, that ringing affirmation may resonate throughout a lifetime.

The poet Peter Meinke may have spoken for many adults when he wrote to his son Peter, age 10:

I thought you knew
you were beautiful and fair
your bright eyes and hair
but now I see that no one knows that
about himself, but must be told
and retold until it takes hold...

The rite presents the opportunity to tell and retell that message. But it gives our words a greater dimension. *God* chooses this child for all eternity. *God* calls this child by name.

Enrollment of Names

Before the rite, draw attention to all the times you or the child sign your name: on checks, receipts, letters, homework, contracts, tests, rental agreements, library cards, etc. Ask:

• What does it mean when we sign our names?

Stress that by signing our names, we commit ourselves: we have put our lives, our time and our integrity on the line. During the rite, signing the name is a promise to commit to a way of life.

During the rite, observe closely and, if possible, put your arm around the shoulders to show support as the child writes his or her name in the book. Richelle Pearl-Koller describes the effort it takes, especially for young children, to complete their signatures: "Inscribing their name is like searing their memory with the great effort needed to live the gospel of Jesus."

After the rite, children like seeing their names in the book of the elect. The parish's record will probably contain many names stretching before the child's, and many will come after. Children love saying, "Here's my name! I belong!" In the book, their response to God's call takes tangible form and is permanently enshrined.

The Elect of God

If your child has experience of political elections, you can make a comparison to the rite: "Just as the people chose X to be our president or Y to be our mayor, so God has chosen you." Stress that this makes the child special. In the words of the rite, "God is always faithful to those [God] calls."

This "vote of confidence" in the child should encourage him or her to continue to live the gospel way of life. Furthermore, it calls on the parents and godparents to be good models whose example will help the children understand what it means to be faithful to Christ.

Follow up the rite afterward by using this prayer over the elect, which some celebrants will use during the rite. Extend your hands over the child or touch the shoulders as you pray:

Lord God,
you created us

and you give us life.
Bless these children
and add them to your family.
May they be joyful in the life you won for us
through Christ our Lord. *Amen.*

Presentation of the Creed

While this presentation usually occurs after the first scrutiny (in Lent), some parishes do it during the catechumenate because Lent is a relatively short period of time.

The ancient Latin term for "presentation" is *traditio* or tradition. The root word means handing on, just as a parent might give an heirloom to a child. If your family proudly passes on such treasures, begin by making the comparison: just as we give you Grandma's china or portrait, so we hand on our beliefs. Point out that the Teutonic word *lief* (as in belief) means love; these things are dear to us.

In preparation for the rite, discuss:
• What promises did you make when you joined the Scouts? 4H Club? Any other group to which you belong?
• Why do you think the church has a set of promises?

After reading the Apostles' Creed or Nicene Creed, explain your own belief by completing this sentence for the child:
• "One phrase of the Creed that especially moves me is... because..."

Invite the child to think through the religious beliefs he or she holds most dear.
• For younger children, ask them to finish the sentence "I believe...," then to fill a sheet of paper with illustrations of those beliefs.
• For older children, pretend that a computer glitch has wiped out all existing creeds. Ask them to compose their own. They may want to design a book with one belief on each page, written in calligraphy or a special computer font.

Presentation of the Our Father

This presentation usually occurs after the third scrutiny, but may also occur during the catechumenate. Remember that children from other

Christian traditions may already be fond of this prayer, so present it with sensitivity.

In preparation for the rite, you might divide the prayer into separate phrases and take turns with the child, explaining what each phrase means to each of you personally.

To follow up after the rite, choose one of these activities:
- Illustrate each of the separate phrases discussed above.
- Learn the prayer in a different language, including sign language.
- Talk about:
  — Why do you think Jesus used this prayer?
  — How could it make a difference in our lives if we prayed this prayer every day?

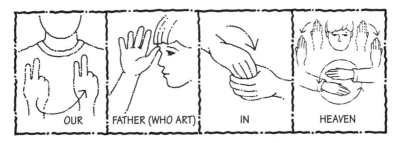

Minor Rites

These rites are celebrated throughout the catechumenate, during the catechetical sessions where the group breaks open the word. They can also be turned into family rituals at home.

Blessing

A blessing is a way of saying, "May you have all the good things God wants for you." In some cultures, parents bless children before they leave home for school or play outside or go to bed. You can bless the child in your care by making the sign of the cross on the forehead while praying, "May the Lord bless you and keep you." Doing this frequently can contribute greatly to the child's self-esteem and security.

You may also invite children to write or draw their own blessings, giving them an example such as this Celtic blessing:

Bless to me, O God,
the earth beneath my foot,
Bless to me, O God,
the path on which I go.

Anointing

This tradition has ancient roots. Prophets, priests and kings were anointed as a sign of their holy calling. The first anointing of the children will probably be done by a priest or deacon with the oil of catechumens. You can continue this practice at home by using a mixture of olive oil and perfume. You may choose a special time to anoint, perhaps at bedtime, at prayer time or at a birthday celebration. Anointing the child will prepare him or her for anointing at the Easter Vigil, where he or she will be lavishly anointed with perfumed chrism (holy oil).

If your child likes historical detail or is fascinated by royalty, you might explain that a secret formula was used to prepare the precious oils and exquisite perfumes for the coronation of Queen Elizabeth II of England. The amber-colored oil included orange flowers, roses, cinnamon, jasmine, musk, ambergris. You may use the same words proclaimed by the archbishop of Canterbury as he anointed the queen beneath a golden canopy:

Be thy hands anointed with holy oil, be thy breast anointed with holy oil, be thy head anointed with holy oil, as kings, priests, prophets were anointed.

You may want to perform the gesture more simply, making the sign of the cross on the child's forehead or hands and saying:

I anoint you (*Name*) with the oil of gladness.

In any form, the anointing is a powerful sign that the child is the precious daughter or son of God. Children who know that the oil poured over them is rare and expensive begin to understand how unique and important they are.

Laying on of Hands

Jesus often touched the people he healed, and he seemed to especially like to touch children (Mark 9:36-37, 10:13-16). While children should be sensitized to inappropriate touching, they still long for the affectionate touch of a parent or significant adult. You may do this simply by putting your arm around the child's shoulders and praying, "Take special care of (*Name*), dear God, for (*she/he*) is precious to me." It takes two minutes, but it offers children powerful affirmation.

Minor Exorcisms

Don't think of some horrible drooling scene from the movie *The Exorcist*. Instead, think of this as a prayer to strengthen Christians against the real evils that surround us. Genuine belief does not have a "pie in the sky," "whistle in the dark" attitude denying evil. The authentic Christian witness knows that child abuse, injustice, disease and assaults on the innocent are rampant in our world. We turn to Christ to strengthen and protect us. Here is a prayer of exorcism, adapted for children from #94 H in the *Rite of Christian Initiation of Adults*. Extend your hands over the child or touch the shoulders as you pray:

> Lord Jesus,
> we pray for (*Name the child*),
> whose ears and heart are open to your word
> like a bird with a mouth that is open.
> Help her to grasp your moment of grace.
> Do not let her heart be troubled.
> Let her know the hope of your promise.
> Fill her with the joy of knowing you. *Amen.*

Another example is adapted from *RCIA* #94 F:

> Lord Jesus Christ,
> we pray for your child (*Name*)
> Show her your mercy
> heal her wounds
> fill her heart with your peace.
> May she delight in discovering your word
> and generously follow your call. *Amen.*

Praying with Scripture

Continue the suggestions for praying with scripture given in the precatechumenate guidebook. This will help the child enter more deeply into the word, proclaimed and broken open on Sunday, that is forming and transforming its hearers. For instance, one family returned home after hearing the story of the wedding feast at Cana (John 2:1-12, the gospel for the Second Sunday in Ordinary Time, Year C). They talked about the places in their lives and in their world that need the touch of Jesus to turn water into wine.

They wrote these concerns (such as child abuse, poverty, war, hunger, disease) on a piece of construction paper and glued it to an empty milk jug. The youngest child held it up as all prayed:
• "Jesus, we have no more wine. Bring us the joy of your presence. *Amen.*"

In *The Religious Potential of the Child*, Sofia Cavalletti writes about children who responded to Jesus' description of himself as the Good Shepherd (John 10:11-16). One little girl being treated for cancer, hospitalized far from her family, cried often but said nothing. Hearing the parable, she responded to the way Jesus calls each sheep by name. Later, the nurse heard her singing happily to herself, "He knows my name."

A disabled twelve-year-old repeated over and over, "Do not be afraid; you lack nothing" and "He is for me alone!" Despite difficulty in speaking, he managed through these words to communicate his great secret to his younger brother.

Ask your child if there is one phrase from the Sunday scripture that he or she would like to memorize and carry throughout the week. Then write it on an index card and hang it where you will both see it often. Or tuck it into the child's pillow so he or she can repeat it, falling asleep.

Listening Prayer

At times invite the child to join you for silent meditation, a few moments of listening to Jesus. At first the silence may seem awkward, but stay with it. Most people today have little silence in their lives because the television or radio is blaring constantly. An inner quiet responds to the Lord's call: "Be still and know that I am God." God wants to speak with us; to hear God's voice we create a responsive attitude of welcome in ourselves and our children.

One way to enter silent prayer is by repeating to oneself a name for God or Jesus: for instance, Creator, Brother, Friend, Holy One, Good Shepherd, Healer, Life-Giver, Prince of Peace."

Activities for Advent, Christmas and Epiphany

"Life is a rich and happy time when one
is waiting for something to happen."
—E. B. White

The period of catechumenate can occur at any time during the year. But as a way of organizing the seasons of the church calendar, this series places activities for Advent, Christmas and Epiphany in this book; activities for Lent in *A Practical Guide to Purification and Enlightenment;* and activities for Easter and Pentecost in *A Practical Guide to Mystagogy.*

Cause for Celebration

Children's days can be dull. Repeatedly, they follow the same orbit of school, playground and home. Of course stability is important, but everyone likes variety in the secure routine.

That's one fringe benefit of the Catholic tradition. The church year is rich in seasons and cycles, balancing feasts and fasts, highs and lows. There is almost always something to celebrate. As the mystic Hildegard of Bingen wrote in the fourteenth century, "Be not lax in celebrating. Be not lazy in the festive service of God. Be ablaze with enthusiasm."

The first place children learn to celebrate is at home, where they blow out the candles on the birthday cake and sing the Christmas carols. In church, children may stare at the backs of heads and hear language they don't understand. At home, they can be active participants: finding a lovely flower or shell as the focal point for prayer, lighting the candles on the Advent wreath, reading the gospel, praying spontaneously, choosing a song.

Parents with tight schedules might worry how they can squeeze in one more thing, but these celebrations need not be long or complicated. Gradually giving the child responsibility for the preparation instills a sense of ownership and relieves some of the burden on mom or dad's time. Nielsen surveys found that the average American household watches television for over 25 hours a week. Surely a few moments for a religious observance can be a more rewarding use of time.

As we have seen repeatedly, adult modeling is crucial. If the children see us joyously absorbed in the celebration, they know it is important for them to participate too. Their radar is set for interesting stuff: if we show enthusiasm and enjoyment, it becomes contagious.

Major Feasts
The First Sunday of Advent usually occurs during the last week of November or the first week of December. The Advent season extends through four weeks, culminating in Christmas. Most years, the feast of Jesus' birth is followed by the Feasts of the Holy Family, Mary the Mother of God, and Epiphany (see below).

Minor Feasts
In between the major feasts are sprinkled lots of interesting opportunities for celebration. Don't be intimidated by this list; simply choose from it a few dates that will work for your family. A suggestion for celebrating the feast follows its name.

11/30—Feast of St. Andrew, who brought his friends to Jesus. Today, remember a friend with a phone call or card.

12/3—Feast of St. Francis Xavier. This Jesuit missionary preached to the Hindus, Malayans and Japanese. On a map or globe, find where their modern descendants might live. Francis respected their unique cultures; borrow a library book on how they live today.

12/6—St. Nicholas Day. Children who put their shoes outside their doors the night before find candy and small toys there in the morning.

They can also be "little Nicholases," secretly doing kindnesses for each other.

12/8—Feast of the Immaculate Conception. We celebrate that Mary was filled with grace from her conception, and thus suited for the unique role in human salvation that would be hers. In honor of Jesus' mother, pray together her hymn of praise, the Magnificat (Luke 1:46-55).

12/12—Feast of Our Lady of Guadalupe. Read the children's version of the story by Tomie dePaola: *The Lady of Guadalupe*.

12/13—Feast of St. Lucy, whose name means light. Adapt the Swedish custom of the oldest daughter wearing a crown of candles and carrying a tray of breakfast rolls to her family the morning of the feast.

12/16—Las Posadas. For the nine days before Christmas, Spanish-speaking people re-enact Mary and Joseph's quest for a place their child could be born. The procession is denied entrance at every home, until at last, one welcomes them and a party with pinatas begins.

12/24—Traditions celebrated on Christmas Eve provide some of the year's most unforgettable moments. Some families have a special reading of the nativity story, others have a special meal; others place a figure of the Christ Child in the crib of the creche.

12/26-1/1—African-Americans celebrate Kwanzaa. On each of the seven days, a candle is lit reaffirming seven principles: unity, self-determination, responsibility, cooperative economics, purpose, creativity and faith.

12/26—St. Stephen's Day. Stephen became the first martyr of the church when he boldly spoke for Jesus and angered the temple authorities. Tell stories of those who speak out boldly in our own day.

12/28—Feast of the Holy Innocents. These little boys were slain by Herod in his murderous attempt to kill the Christ Child. Some European countries call this "Children's Day" and put children in charge of planning activities and games.

12/31—New Year's Eve is a good time to take stock of the past year and especially to thank God for all the blessings it brought.

1/4—Feast of Elizabeth Ann Seton. The widowed mother of five small children, she was the first saint born in the United States to be canonized by the Catholic Church. Two of her daughters died in childhood, but despite her grief, Seton went on to found the first North American parish school, religious community and orphanage. She could be the patron saint of single parents.

A moveable feast also occurs during this season: Hanukkah, the Eight Day Festival of Lights. In the Jewish tradition, families light the menorah, one candle each night for eight nights, and play games with dreidels or spinning tops.

Advent Activities
Straw in the Crib
One of the simplest preparations for Christmas is for children to fill a small empty crib with straw or small pieces of yellow yarn. Each piece they contribute represents a kindness they have done. Their goal is to soften the bed of the Christ Child when he comes. The crib can be a part of your creche scene. Some families also like to position the crib figures (shepherds, sheep, Magi, camels, etc.) all over the house, allowing the children to move them one step closer to the creche each day of Advent.

Advent Calendar
You may buy a ready-made Calendar or make your own, following either set of directions. The first is more complicated (perhaps better suited to older or more skilled children); the second is simpler.

Advanced Version
• Make a cardboard circle pattern, 3 inches in diameter, or find a jar lid 3 inches wide.

Ask children to cut out 56 3-inch circles from construction paper. Use a black felt pen to number half the circles, 1 through 28.
• From cards, magazines and wrapping paper, children then cut 28 Christmas pictures that could fit inside a 3-inch circle. They glue the pictures onto the unnumbered circles.

- Write *Jesus Is Coming* at the top of a large poster board. Have the children glue the circles with pictures onto the poster board. Then, using small pieces of tape, they cover each picture with one of the numbered circles. The numbers need not go sequentially; sometimes they are more fun to find when scattered around the poster.
- Each day of Advent, children can remove one of the numbered circles to reveal the picture underneath. This provides a regular opportunity to talk about the coming of Jesus and how they are getting ready for his birth.

Easier Version
- Ask children each to choose two sheets of construction paper, one light and one dark.
- Children tear a large shape from the lighter sheet: a circle, an arch, a diamond...
- On a piece of drawing paper, children use chalk dipped in sugar water to draw a picture of the first Christmas. As they work, encourage them to discuss the story, learning its details from each other.
- Glue the finished picture to the darker paper. Glue the lighter paper (the frame) over it, making the opening larger if necessary to see the picture.
- Look at a calendar and count how many days remain until Christmas. Each child should receive the same number of gummed foil stars, perhaps in an envelope. Then the child sticks one star on the frame for every day until Christmas.

Jesse Tree
- Find a bare branch to decorate and anchor it in a large can or vase filled with sand.
- On sturdy colored paper or felt, make symbols of the people who prepared the way for Christ, his and our ancestors in faith:
  — an apple for Adam and Eve
  — a boat for Noah
  — a harp for David
  — a loaf of bread for Sarah
  — a ladder for Jacob
  — a lamb for Isaac
  — a horn for Joshua
  — a tambourine for Miriam

— a scarlet cord for Rahab
— a crown for Solomon
— a lamp for Samuel
— a burning bush for Moses
— a striped coat for Joseph
— a sheaf of wheat for Ruth
— a star of David for Mary

This activity can be extended over several weeks, maybe making one symbol a day.

• Cut out the symbol and punch a hole in it. Insert thread or ribbon through the hole and hang it from the branch.
• If you can, read the story about the person, found in the Old Testament, as you hang the symbol.

JOSEPH   NOAH   MARY   RUTH

Advent Wreath

• Begin with a dinner plate or sturdy tray.
• Ask children to make four balls of clay or play dough and space them in a circle around the plate. Insert candles in the balls: either four purple ones, or three purple and one rose-colored candle.
• If you wish, tie ribbon around the bases of the candles.
• Cover the remaining space on the plate or tray with greenery.
• On the First Sunday of Advent, light one candle; on the second, two, and so on. If you use a rose candle, light it on the third Sunday as a symbol of joy.
• Invite children to choose an Advent song such as "O Come, O Come Emmanuel" or "Prepare Ye the Way of the Lord" from *Godspell*. Sing a verse as you light the candles.

- Invite spontaneous prayer by asking:
    Jesus promises to come to us. How can we ask Jesus to come? How does Jesus come today?
- Close by praying:
    Come Lord Jesus, to us who wait for you as Mary waited for you long ago. *Amen.*
- Invite the children to sing again and blow out the candles.

Reverse Suggestion Box
Decorate an empty tissue box with symbols of Advent, or cover it in Christmas wrapping. Inside the box, put slips of paper on which family members have written kind deeds. For example: take out the trash, read someone a story, send a card or note, set the table, pack lunches. Each day, each person draws out one paper and follows the suggestion on it.

Pyramid of Light—A Decoration
Join three red apples with dowels or chop sticks. These form a triangular base for a fourth apple, held aloft by three sticks to the apples at the base. Place a candle in the stem of each apple.

Christmas Books
A wide variety of books for children can enrich this season. Choose age-appropriate ones, borrow from your local library and enjoy reading together at bedtime. Or buy a book to include in a St. Nicholas's shoe or a Christmas stocking: better than candy!

Julie Vivas, *The Nativity*

Marie Hall Ets, *Nine Days 'til Christmas*

Barbara Berger, *The Donkey's Dream*

Norma Farber, *All Those Mothers at the Stable*

Isabelle Brent, *The Christmas Story*

Tomie dePaola, *The First Christmas, The Three Wise Kings*

Laura Ingalls Wilder, "Mr. Edwards Meets Santa Claus" in *Little House on the Prairie*

Jan Pienkowski, *Christmas*

Rebecca Caudill, *A Certain Small Shepherd*

Barbara Robinson, *The Best Christmas Pageant Ever*

Feast of Mary, Mother of God

January 1
Read Luke 2:16-21, the gospel for this feast.

Reflect on the way Mary "treasured" the shepherds' words and "pondered them in her heart." Ask children:

* When we treasure something, how do we feel about it?
* What do you treasure?
* What does it mean to treasure words as Mary did? Are there any special words that you treasure?
* Write these words (perhaps some from scripture) on hearts cut from construction paper, illustrating them if you like. Then hang them on a wall or string them to make a mobile.

Blessing for the New Year

adapted from *Catholic Household Blessings and Prayers*

(A family member may hold a calendar of the new year during the blessing.)

Leader: Let us praise the Lord of days and seasons and years, saying: "Glory to God in the highest!"

All: And peace to all people on earth!

Leader: Our lives are made of days and nights, of seasons and years, for we are part of a universe of suns and moons and planets. We mark ends and we make beginnings and, in all, we praise God for the grace and mercy that fill our days.

(A scripture passage such as Genesis 1:14-19 or Psalm 90:1-4 may be read.)

Parents place their hands on their children's heads in blessing as the *leader* says:

Remember us, O God;
from age to age be our comforter.
You have given us the wonder of time,
blessings in days and nights, seasons and years.
Bless your children at the turning of the year

and fill the months ahead with the bright hope
that is ours in the coming of Christ.
You are our God, living and reigning, forever and ever. *Amen.*

Today is also a day of prayer for world peace. With children, you might pray St. Francis's prayer for peace (in *Children and Christian Initiation: A Practical Guide to the Precatechumenate*, p. 15) or use the Native American "Prayer for Peace," sung on David Haas's audiocassette, "As Water to the Thirsty":

Peace before us
Peace behind us
Peace under our feet.
Peace within us
Peace over us
Let all around us be peace.

Feast of the Holy Family

First Sunday after Christmas
You may want to pray this blessing after Mass or at mealtime.

Blessing for a Family or Household
adapted from *Catholic Household Blessings and Prayers*

Leader: The grace of our Lord Jesus Christ be with us all, now and for ever.

All: Amen.

Leader: We are a family. For one another, we are love and trial, strength and trouble. Even when far apart, we belong to one another and, in various ways, we remember and pray for one another. We join now to give thanks to God and to ask God's blessing on this family.

All: In good times and in bad,
   in sickness and in health,
   we belong to each other
   as we belong to you, God ever faithful.

   By morning and by night
   may your name be on our lips,

a blessing to all our days:
so may kindness and patience be ever among us,
a hunger for justice,
and songs of thankfulness in all we do.

We ask this through Christ our Lord. *Amen.*

The leader can sprinkle all with holy water, or each person can take holy water and make the sign of the cross.

Epiphany

January 6, or the Sunday between January 2 and January 8
Your child may participate in a formal session on Epiphany. Here are some ways to follow up on the session or to celebrate the feast at home.

- The Magi found Jesus in a house, the ordinary setting where most of us live out our days. His presence in our homes makes them holy places. To symbolize the sacred in the ordinary, bless the home today. Have a child lead the procession, perhaps carrying a candle. At each room, pause to have family members say why this space is sacred. Then sprinkle the room with holy water, saying something like this: "Peace be with this house and with all who live here."
- Cut an apple in half and let children find the star pattern inside.
- Cut a star shape from yellow construction paper. Place it on top of a pad of newspaper and a sheet of wax paper. Then sprinkle the star with glitter and crayon shavings. Place a second sheet of wax paper over the star. Cover it with another sheet of newspaper. Then (with adult supervision) iron the star. The crayon and wax paper will melt, sealing the glittering, colorful star inside. The star can be hung in a window at home, or used for the "Star Track" activity (below) during the week.
- Prepare for a "Star Track" with your family in the week after Epiphany. With the children, make a star and decorate it (above). Then each "wise person" in the family does something special for another person, such as making a bed, straightening a shelf, sewing on a button. He or she leaves the star "at the scene." The next person to find the star does something special in turn, leaving the star.

Commitment to Service

"No one has a right to sit down and feel
hopeless. There's too much work to do."
—Dorothy Day

An interviewer once questioned a young woman about why she had volunteered two years of her life as one of the first Peace Corps members. "I'd never done anything political, patriotic or unselfish because nobody ever asked me to," she answered. "Kennedy asked."

During the catechumenate it is your job to *ask*, to call the child forth for service. The formation of this period occurs through the word and the minor rites. To condense the mystery of rite, symbol and story into a single message could oversimplify. But despite that risk, it is still possible to say that the child hears repeatedly in various ways, "You are graced and important. Gift others with the blessings you have received."

Models of Service

A model for this call to children is Zacchaeus, whose story is found in Luke 19. Zacchaeus was so fascinated by Jesus that he climbed a sycamore tree to see him better. Jesus openly welcomed Zacchaeus and invited himself to stay at his home. After spending time with Jesus, Zacchaeus could see his own life differently. He promised the Lord he would give half his possessions to the poor and would repay fourfold anyone he had defrauded. The light of Jesus gave him a different lens to use for the rest of his life. Thus Jesus proclaimed, "Today salvation has come to this house."

Jesus still has that effect on people. Rita Burns Senseman describes Antonio, a member of her parish initiation group, who was shy and withdrawn when he began the process. He became outgoing and involved, an active member of the youth group. He and his mom could be counted on to work regularly at the parish pancake breakfasts that benefited needy families. After meeting Jesus, no one remains the same. Like the child who offered Jesus five barley loaves and several fish, even our smallest efforts can be multiplied by his power.

Faith in Action

By spending time with Jesus and his word, the children are gradually formed in an attitude of mission. Furthermore, the actions of the community model that service is an important part of their Christian commitment. While a Gallup poll showed 89.2 million Americans volunteering 19.5 billion hours of their time in 1993, a faith component gives staying power to that altruism. Those who serve "for the long haul" attribute their dedication to a life of prayer and a religious inspiration.

The concept of Christian service is broad: not confined to the parish (singing in the choir or being a eucharistic minister), but leavening the larger world where most people live out their commitments (being a faithful spouse, acting with integrity on the job). It could be as simple as a lady who got off the bus and asked a bystander when another bus was due. "But you just got off that one!" he retorted. "Well," she explained, "there was a terribly crippled man on that bus and no one offered him a seat. I knew he'd be embarrassed if an old lady like me offered him her seat. So I pretended this was my stop."

The model of such Christians in action says more to children than any book or homily. As children learn more about Jesus, they see him curing the blind, dining with the rejected, helping the paralyzed to walk. He promises his followers that they will do even greater things.

Sometimes, however, we fail to recognize these works. Do we underestimate the daily sacrifices of parents, the fidelity of people who grow our food, collect our trash, clean our streets, repair our cars, and provide our education and medical care? Perhaps the first step toward service is sensitizing children to the evidence of it that surrounds us.

Opportunities to observe service in action might be as simple as taking the child to work with you for a day, or arranging for the child to accompany one of your friends. Through the parish, you and the child may have opportunities to visit and volunteer at a homeless shelter, a soup kitchen, a hospital or a day care center. Families who work together on service projects find that the shared commitment binds them in a unique way.

These direct experiences are preferable to any talk or study about social issues. An experienced campus minister writes, "We can have all the social encyclicals and pastoral statements we want...but who reads them? A handful of folks. Put a student from a middle-class family...into a St. Vincent de Paul pantry for one working session, then bring those students back and have a reflection time with them. You will find that they have been more impacted by what they did rather than what is available on their religious-center library shelf."

Practical Ways to Start Service

Leading an individual child to service is something of a balancing act. While you want to sensitize the child to the needs of others, you do not want the needs to seem so overwhelming that the child becomes paralyzed. With the child, reflect on the question:

• How can we demonstrate the kindness of Christ to those who yearn for it?

One Day in the Lives of America's Children
The following statistics were collected by the Children's Defense Fund in 1991; the situation has grown worse since then. During one typical day:

• 105 babies die before their first birthday
• 27 children die from poverty
• 3 children die from child abuse
• 6 teenagers commit suicide
• 1,849 children are abused or neglected
• 100,000 children are homeless

Children can become informed about global issues through videos and programs offered by Catholic Relief Services, Bread for the World and other agencies. But "a journey of a thousand miles begins with a single step." For most children, forming an attitude is the first step that starts close to home. With your help, children can:

- Participate in parish programs such as Loaves and Fishes, supporting a soup kitchen or stocking a food bank. Emphasize those that help children their own age.
- Help cook a simple, meatless meal once a week at home and contribute the money saved to a program that alleviates hunger.
- Volunteer service in their neighborhood, school or home:
  — Mow lawns, shovel walks, weed gardens, baby-sit, walk neighbors' pets, pick up litter, clean graffiti, help younger siblings with homework—without charge.
  — Arrange for classes at school, scout troops or athletic teams to collect trial-sized toiletries for a homeless shelter.
  — Have the same groups collect toys, puzzles, books, tapes, etc., for the children in a battered women's shelter.
  — Have their families adopt a "grandparent," an elderly person who needs transportation to church, doctor appointments, etc., or would enjoy being included in family activities.
  — Have their families "adopt" a high school or college-aged transfer student from another country who would like to participate in family outings, meals, etc.

Conversations About Service

These questions can prompt a discussion with a child about mission or service:

  — How can a person your age make a difference in someone else's life?
  — Whom do you admire for their efforts to serve others? Why?
  — Why is it important to live a life of service?
  — What do the gospel stories say about service?

If it is possible for the child to observe or interview someone who is active in ministry, discuss afterward:

  — What is this person's ministry?
  — What does he or she like best about his or her ministry?
  — What's the one thing you'll remember about this person?
  — Do you want to be like him or her?

A Practical Guide to the Catechumenate

Possible Service Projects

Opportunities for service will vary widely in different circumstances and locations. This list is not meant to be definitive, but to suggest similar projects that might be available in your own areas.

International and National

Catholic Relief Services

209 W. Fayette St.

Baltimore, MD 21201-3443

1-800-222-0025

> Provides videos on hunger issues, suitable for different age groups, material for Operation Rice Bowl during Lent.

Bread for the World

802 Rhode Island Ave., NE

Washington, D.C. 20018

(202) 684-1196

> Offers study guides, pamphlets, dramas, games and videos about hunger. Also needs letter-writers to impact public policy on hunger issues.

Heifer Project

P.O. Box 808

Little Rock, AR 72203

> Gives livestock to poor families, who in turn share an offspring of that animal with another poor family.

Amnesty International

304 W. 58th St.

New York, NY 10019

(212) 583-4440

> Invites participation in writing letters to help free people unjustly imprisoned by oppressive regimes.

Habitat for Humanity

121 Habitat St.

Americus, GA 31709

(912)924-6935

Offers opportunities to help in building low-cost homes for the homeless: painting, hammering, sawing, providing lunch for other volunteers.

Local

Participate in a CROP walk for the hungry or help with a gleaning project (harvesting surplus produce for the hungry).

Hold a youth lock-in or fast for 24 hours. Catholic Relief Services (above) can provide a step-by-step program.

Call the Catholic Worker soup kitchen or your local homeless shelter or battered women's shelter to ask how you could help out.

Collect unused toys or clothing; ask your local Catholic Community Services where to donate them.

Recycle cans, newspaper, plastic and glass; give the money (anonymously) to a family in the parish that needs it.

Your thoughts on service or ideas for projects:

_____

_____

_____

_____

_____

_____